Made in America

Written by Claire Owen

U.S.A.

My name is Keisha, and I live in New York. I like to play Monopoly® with my cousins and Scrabble® with my mom. What is your favorite board game? Do you know when and where it was invented?

Contents

Wherever you see me, you'll find activities to try and questions to answer.

Made in America

Some toys and games date back hundreds or even thousands of years. More recently, the development of new technologies and materials has led to the invention of many toys and games around the world. LEGO® was invented in Denmark and Rubik's Cube in Hungary; Trivial Pursuit® came from Canada and Nintendo® from Japan. Many of the world's most popular toys, games, and amusements, however, were invented and manufactured in America.

LEGO® bricks can be used to build amazing models.
This LEGO® man is from LEGOLAND® in Germany.

Some Toys, Games, and Amusements Invented in America

Year	Item	Year	Item
1889	Flexible Flyer sled	1956	Ant farm
1896	Comic books	1957	Frisbee®
1901	Electric train	1958	Hula-Hoop®
1902	Teddy bear	1958	Skateboard
1913	Tinkertoy®	1959	Barbie®
1915	Raggedy Ann doll	1960	Etch A Sketch®
1916	Lincoln Logs®	1963	GI Joe®
1917	Little Red Wagon	1965	Super Ball®
1919	Pogo stick	1966	Twister®
1933	Monopoly®	1970	NERF® Ball
1945	Slinky®	1971	Pong
1946	Tonka® Trucks	1972	Uno®
1948	Scrabble®	1983	Cabbage Patch Kids®
1950	Silly Putty®	1983	Care Bears™
1952	Mr. Potato Head®	1993	Beanie Babies®

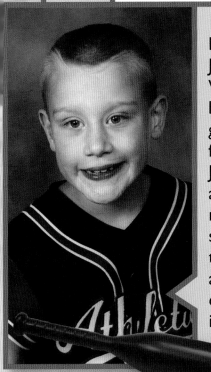

In 2000, six-year-old Jacob Dunnack from Willimantic, Connecticut, brought his bat to his grandma's house but forgot to bring his ball. Jacob, who is sight-impaired and has limited use of his right arm, set about making sure that other kids didn't leave their baseballs behind. He created a hollow, plastic baseball bat with a removable cap so baseballs could be stored inside. Jacob's invention is called the JD Batball.

Pick two items from the list. How many years apart were they invented? Which items were invented 104 years apart? ... 25? ... 51? ... 19? ... 67 years apart?

Monopoly® Millionaire

During the Great Depression of the 1930s, Charles B. Darrow, an unemployed salesman from Pennsylvania, showed a board game called Monopoly® to Parker Brothers, a manufacturer of games and toys. Parker Brothers rejected Monopoly®, telling Darrow that it had 52 flaws! However, after Darrow sold 5,000 handmade sets, Parker Brothers executives changed their minds. In 1935, Monopoly® became the best-selling board game in America, and soon Charles Darrow was a millionaire.

Charles Darrow

depression   a time when business is bad and many people lose their jobs

Monopoly® Trivia

- Since 1935, more than 200 million Monopoly® sets have been sold. This makes Monopoly® the world's best-selling board game.

- More than 500 million people have played Monopoly®.

- About 50 billion dollars' worth of Monopoly® money is printed each year.

- The world's most expensive Monopoly® set is valued at $2 million. The board is gold plated, and the solid-gold houses, hotels, and dice are set with diamonds, rubies, and sapphires!

Monopoly® World Championships

Figure It Out

1. The number of bills of each denomination in a standard Monopoly® set is—

$500	$100	$50	$20	$10	$5	$1
20	20	30	50	40	40	40

What is the total amount of money supplied?

2. Each player starts with—

$500	$100	$50	$20	$10	$5	$1
2	2	2	6	5	5	5

How much money is that?

3. After the players have received their starting amounts, how much money would be left in the bank if there were—

   a. 2 players?   c. 4 players?

   b. 3 players?   d. 5 players?

4. Use information from the Monopoly® Trivia column on the left to make up a problem for the class to solve.

An International Game

The original version of Monopoly® was set in Atlantic City, New Jersey. Today, there are versions of Monopoly® set in cities and countries all around the world, including London, Paris, and Australia. Monopoly® is published in 26 languages and is sold in 80 countries. Large-scale Monopoly® boards have also been created for special events.

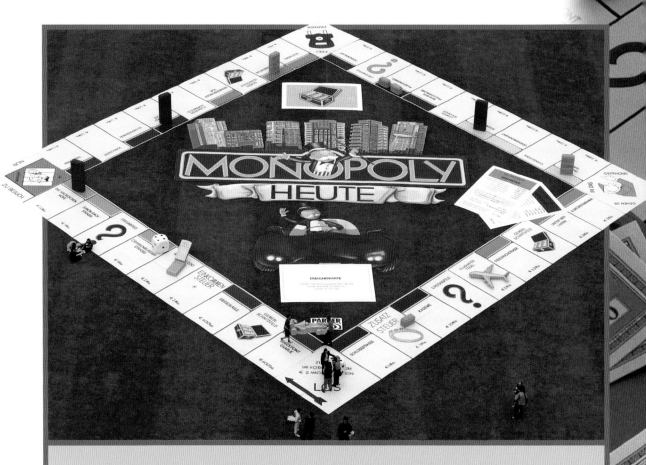

New collector's editions of the classic game were released in 2005 to celebrate Monopoly's® 70th anniversary. In the same year, Monopoly® was played on this giant board in Berlin, Germany.

More Monopoly® Trivia

- Largest permanent Monopoly® board (San Jose, California): 31 feet by 31 feet

- Largest outdoor board: 938 feet by 765 feet

- Largest indoor board: 122 feet by 122 feet

- Longest Monopoly® game: 1,680 hours

- Longest underwater game (played by 350 divers who took turns using a board that weighed 95 pounds): 1,080 hours

- Records have been set for playing Monopoly® upside down (36 hours), in a tree house (286 hours), underground (100 hours), and in a bathtub (99 hours)!

Estimate and then calculate the area of each of the large Monopoly® boards. Convert each of the record playing times into days and hours.

Divers hoping to set a record used specially weighted game pieces and a special board to play Monopoly® underwater.

Lucky Letters

Scrabble®, the world's most popular word game, was invented by another person who was unemployed during the Great Depression. Alfred Mosher Butts originally called his new game *Criss-Cross Words*. Butts analyzed how often each letter of the alphabet appeared on the front page of the *New York Times*. That helped him to decide on the number of tiles for each letter and the value of each letter in his word game.

Alfred Mosher Butts

Scrabble® championships, like the one shown above in Australia, are now held in many countries around the world.

Letter Frequencies

	Average Percent in Text (%)	Number of Scrabble® Tiles (Out of 100)
A	8.2	9
B	1.5	2
C	2.8	2
D	4.3	4
E	12.7	12
F	2.2	2
G	2.0	3
H	6.1	2
I	7.0	9
J	0.2	1
K	0.8	1
L	4.0	4
M	2.4	2
N	6.7	6
O	7.5	8
P	1.9	2
Q	0.1	1
R	6.0	6
S	6.3	4
T	9.1	6
U	2.8	4
V	1.0	2
W	2.4	2
X	0.2	1
Y	2.0	2
Z	0.1	1

Did You Know?

Scrabble® is available in more than 30 languages, including Braille. The letters represented on the tiles, and the number of points each letter is worth, varies from language to language. Spanish Scrabble®, for example, includes tiles that show Ñ, LL, CH, and RR. Hungarian Scrabble® has 38 different tiles! Polish Scrabble® has five Zs, each worth one point.

For each letter, compare the number of tiles in a Scrabble® set and the average percent in text. For how many letters is the difference more than 1.0?

Scrabble® Success

Unable to interest toy companies in Criss-Cross Words,
Alfred Butts began making the game himself, by hand. In 1948,
his business partner, James Brunot, renamed the game Scrabble®.
The following year, Brunot manufactured 2,400 Scrabble®
sets but lost $450. In 1952, however, the game "took off,"
and more than 4 million sets were sold in two years!
Today, about 5 million sets are sold annually.

James Brunot

About how
many Scrabble® sets
were produced each week
in 1949? Today, about
how many sets are
sold each week?

In 1998, the British Army and Navy competed against each other in literally the biggest game of Scrabble® in the world. The "board" measured 103 feet along each side.

Each year, some 200 middle-school students from around the U.S. compete in the National School Scrabble® Tournament.

Figure It Out

Z_{10} E_1 B_3 R_1 A_1

1. Find the score for the word *ZEBRA* if—
   a. the letter *E* is on a double-word square.
   b. *Z* and *B* are each on a double-letter square.
   c. *Z* is on a double-letter square and *A* is on a double-word square.
   d. *Z* is on a triple-word square and *A* is on a double-letter square.
   e. *Z* and *A* are each on a triple-letter square.

Q_{10} U_1 I_1 V_4 E_1 R_1 S_1

2. The word *QUIVERS* was joined to *ZEBRA*, also making *ZEBRAS*. The letter *Q* was on a triple-word square, and the letter *V* was on a double-letter square.

What was the total score? (Count both words and add a bonus of 50 points for playing all seven letters.)

The Hula-Hoop® Craze

Children around the world have played with hoops for thousands of years. In the 18th century, sailors visiting Hawaii noticed the similarity between hula dancing and the movements people made when twirling a hoop around their waist. The Hula-Hoop® was reinvented in 1957 by the founders of the Wham-O Company. The company sold more than 100 million plastic hoops in two years!

In 1958, it seemed that every child had a Hula-Hoop®!

Hula-Hoop® Marathon Records*

Time (Hours)	Date
11	August 1976
25	June 1978
54	October 1978
60	July 1983
72	October 1984
88	July 1986
90	April 1987

*Twirling a hoop nonstop, in between the shoulders and the hips

Record Number of Hula-Hoops®*

Number	Date
58	April 1975
62	October 3, 1976
63	April 1, 1979
75	April 7, 1982
81	September 19, 1983
82	September 3, 1994
83	October 25, 1999
85	January 6, 2001
90	April 10, 2002
95	April 8, 2003

*Twirling at the same time, from a stationary start

American Lori Lynn Lomeli is a champion Hula-Hoop® twirler. She is shown here simultaneously swinging 83 Hula-Hoops® a total of three times.

Suppose that the 90-hour Hula-Hoop® marathon began at 10 A.M. on April 2, 1987. When did the marathon end?

simultaneously   at the same time

15

Twirling Circles

Hula-Hoops® come in three standard sizes, with a diameter of 24 inches, 30 inches, or 36 inches. However, Paul "Dizzy Hips" Blair used a hoop with a diameter of 13.8 feet to break the world record for twirling the largest hoop! Blair managed to make at least three revolutions of the huge hoop on June 21, 2003. He also broke two other world records on the same day.

On October 28, 2000, a new world record was set in Taiwan when 2,469 people simultaneously twirled hoops for two minutes.

diameter   a line segment that joins two points on a circle and passes through the center

Largest Hula-Hoops® Twirled

Diameter (Feet)	Record Holder	Date
10.4	Roman Schedeler (Austria)	May 27, 1995
11.8	Laura Rico Rodriguez (Spain)	December 14, 2001
13.1	Tsuji Nozomi (Japan)	January 1, 2003
13.8	Paul "Dizzy Hips" Blair (U.S.A.)	June 21, 2003

Did You Know?

To find the length of the circumference of a circle, you can multiply the diameter by a special number called pi (π). Pi is approximately equal to 3.14.

Estimate and then calculate the circumference of each of the hoops on pages 16–17. (Round your answers to the nearest tenth of a foot or inch.)

Paul Blair broke the record for running a mile while Hula-Hooping®. He set a new world-record time of 7:47 (7 minutes and 47 seconds). Blair also ran 10 kilometers (6.25 miles) while Hula-Hooping®, achieving a new record time of 1:06:35.

circumference the outer boundary, especially of a circle

Picking Up Sticks

Some popular toys and games were made and played in America long before Europeans arrived in the 1500s. For example, Native Americans used decorated sticks, straws, or pieces of reed to play a variety of games. Some historians think that the game called *Jack Straws* or *Pick-Up Sticks* developed from a game that the Lenape people of Delaware called *Selahtikàn*.

Many versions of Jack Straws have been made in America over the years. There have been magnetic, electric, and glow-in-the-dark Jack Straws!

Playing with Straws

In 1990, Joel Glickman (below) was playing with drinking straws while at a wedding. He soon realized that with the addition of some simple connectors, sticks would make a great building set. After the wedding, Joel followed up his idea with some creative product engineering, and it wasn't long before K'NEX® rod-and-connector building systems were available throughout the world!

Playing Hubbub

Another popular Native American game, often called *Hubbub*, was played with a bowl and five or six "dice." The dice were two-sided discs made from bone, antler, or fruit pits, with one plain side and one decorated side. This game was simple to play, but the scoring system was complex. The dice were placed in a bowl and tossed in the air. Sticks or beans were awarded for certain outcomes.

outcome   in mathematics, a possible result of a random process

Play 10 rounds of Hubbub with a group or partner. (Toss 6 two-color counters in a plastic bowl. Use craft sticks and straws to keep score.)

Simplified Rules for Hubbub

- Players take turns tossing 6 dice in the bowl.
- No sticks are awarded unless 5 or 6 of the dice are alike.
- Players who toss 5 or 6 alike are awarded flat or thin sticks (see below). Then they get a second turn. If they toss the same number again, they are awarded more sticks and get a third turn.

Scoring System

Toss	1st Turn	2nd Turn	3rd Turn
6 alike	1 flat stick	2 flat sticks	3 flat sticks
5 alike	3 thin sticks	9 thin sticks	1 flat stick

Note: One flat stick is worth the same as 16 thin sticks.

Analyzing the Odds

When playing Hubbub with 6 two-color counters, there are
7 possible outcomes:

Number of red	6	5	4	3	2	1	0
Number of yellow	0	1	2	3	4	5	6

However, all of the outcomes are not equally likely. For example,
there is only one way to get 6 red counters:

●●●●●●

… but there are 6 ways to get 5 red counters:

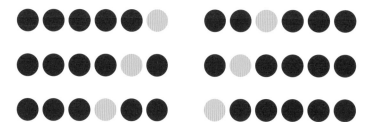

Altogether, there are 64 ways
to toss 6 counters. Only two
of those combinations have
6 counters of the same color.
There are 12 ways to get
5 counters of the same color.

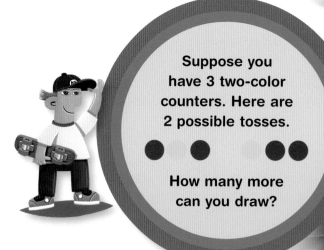

Suppose you
have 3 two-color
counters. Here are
2 possible tosses.

How many more
can you draw?

22

Graph Outcomes for Three Counters

You will need a copy of the Blackline Master, a pencil and paper, 3 two-color counters, a cup, and a colored marker or pencil.

1. Label the graph to show the 4 possible outcomes when you toss 3 two-color counters. Write "3" to complete the title.

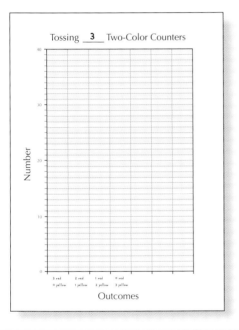

2. Write answers to these questions on a sheet of paper:
- Do you think that all of the outcomes are equally likely? Why or why not?
- About how many of each outcome would you expect to get in 80 tosses?

3. Pour 3 counters out of the cup. Color a box on the grid to show the outcome.

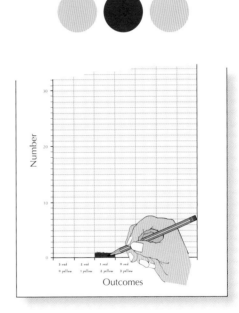

4. Repeat Step 3 until you have colored 80 squares. Then write about your results.
- Did each outcome occur approximately the same number of times?
- Were the results what you expected?

Sample Answers

Do some research about one of the other toys or games on page 5. For example, you could find out about world records related to the Frisbee® or the pogo stick.

Page 5   Answers include:
104 years: 1889–1993
25 years: 1933–58
51 years: 1901–52
19 years: 1896–1915
67 years: 1889–1956

Page 7   1. $15,140   2. $1,500   3. a. $12,140
b. $10,640   c. $9,140   d. $7,640

Page 9   (square feet): 961; 717,570;
14,884; (days and hours): 70:0,
45:0, 1:12, 11:22, 4:4, 4:3

Page 11   5 letters: H, I, S, T, U

Page 12   about 46 sets; about 96,154 sets

Page 13   1. a. 32   b. 29   c. 52   d. 51   e. 38
2. 136

Page 15   4 A.M. on April 6, 1987

Page 17   d (in.)   24   30   36
C (in.)   75.4   94.2   113.0
d (ft)   10.4   11.8   13.1 13.8
C (ft)   32.7   37.1   41.1   43.3

Page 22   6 more: ●●● ● ○○○ ●○○
○○● ○ ○●● ●●○

Index